Dear Mum

from you to me®

from you to me®

GIFTS THAT TOUCH LIVES

Dear Mum

from you to me®

This book is for your Mother's unique and amazing story.

It is for her to capture some of her life's key memories, experiences and feelings.

Ask her to complete it carefully and, if she wants to, add some photographs or images to personalise it more.

When it is finished and returned to you, this will be a record of her story . . . a story that you will treasure forever.

Dear

Here is my letter to you ...

.

Tell me about the time and place you were born . . .

What are your earliest memories?

Tell me about your Mum and Dad . . .

What do you think your parents thought of you as a child?

What interesting **information** do you know about other people in our family?

Please detail what you know of our family tree ...

Here's some space for you to add more about our family that will **interest** generations to come . . .

What do you remember about the place/s you lived when you were a child?

What were your favourite childhood toys or games?

Tell me about your best friend/s as a young child . . .

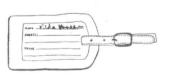

What do you remember about your holidays as a child?

What sort of pets did you have when you were young and what were their names?

What were you best at when you were at school?

What did you want to do when you grew up?

♪ OLIVE TREE FESTIVAL ♪

SATURDAY 17th & SUNDAY 18th JUNE

WEEKEND TICKET

07428

Who was your best friend as a teenager... and why?

What were your favourite hobbies when you were young?

Did you have an idol when you were young?
Tell me who and why . . .

What was the first piece of music you bought?

What piece/s of music would you choose in your own favourite 'top 10' from when you were young?

Describe some of the favourite outfits you wore as a young woman . . .

What age were you when you started work?
Tell me about the jobs you have had . . .

How did you meet my Father?

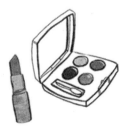

What would you do for a night-out when you were dating?

Tell me about a memorable piece of music that you and Dad had 'just for you'...

Describe the occasion when you first met my Dad's parents . . .

Describe a special day you had with my Father . . .

How did you feel when you found out you were pregnant with me?

What did you think when you first saw me after I was born?

What were my statistics when I was born
. . . time of birth, weight, height etc?

What did I look like when I was born?
If you have a photo, could you stick it here please . . .

What was the first thing my Father said to you after I was born?

What was my nickname before I was born or when I was young?

Before I was born, what other names had you thought of calling me?

What was the first word or words you remember me saying?

Describe some of the favourite memories you have of me when I was a child . . .

What was I like when I was a child?

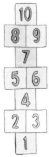

What attributes did I have as a child that I still have now?

What were you most proud of about me when I was at school?

Describe what you like about me . . .

Is there anything you would like to change about me?

What are the happiest or greatest memories of your life?

What are a few of your favourite things?

Describe your memory of some major world events that have happened in your lifetime . . .

Describe the greatest change that you have seen in your lifetime so far . . .

Describe something you still want to achieve in your life . . .

Tell me about the dreams you have for your life . . .

If you were an animal... what type of animal would you be, and why?

If you won the Lottery... what would you do with the money?

What have you found most difficult in your life?

What is your **biggest regret** in your life?

Can you do anything about it **now**?

With hindsight what would you do differently?

Tell me something you think I won't know about you . . .

What would you like your epitaph to say?

Is there anything you would like to say sorry for?

What piece of advice would you like to offer me?

And now your chance to write anything else you want to say to me . . .

These extra pages are for us to write any **questions, memories** or **answers** that may not have been covered elsewhere in the book . . .

And finally for the record . . .

what is your full name ?

what was your maiden name ?

what is your date of birth ?

what colour are your eyes ?

how tall are you ?

what blood group are you ?

what was the date when you completed this story for me ?

And a few words to thank you for completing this Journal of a Lifetime ...

Published by from you to me ltd

All titles are available from good gift and book shops or www.fromyoutome.com

from you to me **Journals of a Lifetime**

Dear Mum
Dear Dad
Dear Grandma
Dear Grandad
Dear Sister
Dear Brother
Dear Daughter
Dear Son
Dear Friend

Parent & Child

Bump to Birthday, pregnancy & first year journal
Our Story, for my daughter
Our Story, for my son
Mum to Mum - pass it on
Dear Baby, guest book

Teen & Tween

Mum & Me
Dad & Me
Rant & Rave - My School
Rant & Rave - My Holiday

Other Titles

Love Stories, anniversary & relationship journal
Cooking up Memories
Digging up Memories
Kicking off Memories
Dear Future Me
These were the Days
Christmas Present, Christmas Past

Personalised

Many of these journals can be personalised online at www.fromyoutome.com

You can also use this code by downloading a free QR code reader app to your smart phone.

Dear Mum

from you to me®

First published in the UK by from you to me, August 2007
Copyright, from you to me limited 2007
Re-designed in January 2012
Hackless House, Murhill, Bath, BA2 7FH
www.fromyoutome.com
E-mail: hello@fromyoutome.com

ISBN 978-1-907048-44-9

Cover design by so design consultants   www.so-design.co.uk

This book is printed on woodfree paper produced from a sustainable source and Elemental Chlorine Free paper sourced to FSC standards. Printed in India by Replika Press on behalf of JFDI print services Ltd.

If you think other questions should be included in future editions, please let us know. And please share some of the interesting answers you receive with us at the from you to me website to let other people read about these fascinating insights . . .

All rights reserved. No part of this publication may be reproduced, stored in a retrieval system or transmitted in any form or by any means, electronic, mechanical, photocopying or otherwise circulated without the publisher's prior consent in any form of binding or cover other than that in which it is published and without a similar condition including this.